SEASONAL ICE COVERAGE

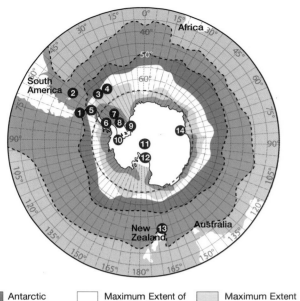

Africa
South America
New Zealand
Australia

■ Antarctic Waters	□ Maximum Extent of Ice in Winter
■ Subantarctic Waters	▨ Maximum Extent of Ice in Spring/Autumn
	▨ Maximum Extent of Ice in Summer

1. Tierra del Fuego
2. Falkland Islands
3. South Georgia
4. South Sandwich Islands
5. South Shetland Islands
6. Antarctic Peninsula
7. Weddell Sea
8. Ronne Ice Shelf
9. Berkner Island
10. Vinson Massif
11. South Pole
12. Ross Ice Shelf
13. Auckland Islands
14. Amery Ice Shelf

The coldest, windiest and driest place on Earth, the Antarctic is one of the toughest places for animals and plants to survive. It supports a handful of birds, a few marine mammals and fish with antifreeze proteins in their blood to help them survive the subzero water temperatures. Plants are rare, with their growth compromised by poor soil quality, lack of sunshine, lack of moisture and freezing temperatures. However, because of its inaccessibility, the Antarctic supports large populations of species that have adapted to the environment. It remains one of the few areas on Earth where many species live their entire lives devoid of human contact.

Most illustrations show the adult male in breeding coloration. Colors and markings may be duller or absent during different seasons. The measurements denote the length of species from bill to tail tip. Illustrations are not to scale.

Waterford Press publishes reference guides that introduce readers to nature observation, outdoor recreation and survival skills. Product information is featured on the website: www.waterfordpress.com

Text & illustrations © 2013, 2023 Waterford Press Inc. All rights reserved. Photos © iStock Photo. To order or for information on custom published products please call 800-434-2555 or email orderdesk@waterfordpress.com. For permissions or to share comments email editor@waterfordpress.com. 2301406

$7.95 U.S.
$9.95 CAN

ISBN 978-1-58355-788-4
9 781583 557884
5 0795

Made in the USA

10 9 8 7 6 5 4 3 2 1

ANTARCTIC WILDLIFE – A Folding Pocket Guide to Familiar Species

ANTARCTIC
WILDLIFE

A Folding Pocket Guide to Familiar Species of the Antarctic and Subantarctic Environments

WATERFORD PRESS

T0123940

PENGUINS

Once classified as fish, penguins are superb swimmers that "fly" underwater. Their legs are set far back on the body to aid in swimming. Of the 18 different species of penguins, only two are true Antarctic residents.

Emperor Penguin
Aptenodytes forsteri
To 4 ft. (1.2 m)
Largest penguin breeds only in Antarctica and is likely the only bird on Earth that never sets foot on land. The only species to breed and incubate it's eggs during the fierce Antarctic winter.

King Penguin
Aptenodytes patagonicus
To 38 in. (95 cm)
Note orange ear patches. Subantarctic species is most common in South Georgia.

Adelie Penguin
Pygoscelis adeliae
To 28 in. (70 cm)
Reddish bill has a black tip. Breeds October-February on shores of the Antarctic continent.

Rockhopper Penguin
Eudyptes chrysocome
To 2 ft. (60 cm)
The smallest polar penguin, it has yellow head plumes that are not joined across the forehead.

Macaroni Penguin
Eudyptes chrysolophus
To 28 in. (70 cm)
Yellow head plumes are joined across the forehead.

Chinstrap Penguin
Pygoscelis antarctica
To 30 in. (75 cm)
Capable of scaling rocky cliffs up to 330 ft. (100 m) high.

Gentoo Penguin
Pygoscelis papua
To 3 ft. (90 cm)
Key field mark is white "bonnet" that runs from eye to eye.

Magellanic Penguin
Spheniscus magellanicus
To 30 in. (75 cm)
Common in South America and the Falkland Islands. Has a braying call and is also called the jackass penguin.

LAND & NEARSHORE BIRDS

These birds are found in southern South America, South Georgia and/or the Falkland Islands.

Upland Goose
Chloephaga picta
To 28 in. (70 cm)
Falklands only.

Ruddy-headed Goose
Chloephaga rubidiceps
To 20 in. (50 cm)
Falklands and South America.

Kelp Goose
Chloephaga hybrida malvinarium
To 27 in. (68 cm)
Falklands resident.

Flightless Steamer Duck
Tachyeres pteneres
To 34 in. (85 cm)
Huge duck with a pugnacious personality.

Yellow-billed Pintail
Anas georgica
To 21 in. (53 cm)
South Georgia only.

Yellow-billed Teal
Anas flavirostris
To 16 in. (40 cm)

Pale-faced Sheathbill
Chionis alba
To 16 in. (40 cm)
Pigeon-like, white shorebird.

Dolphin Gull
Leucophaeus scoresbii
To 18 in. (45 cm)
Bill and legs are red.

Kelp Gull
Larus dominicanus
To 23 in. (58 cm)
Note all-white tail.

Brown-hooded Gull
Chroicocephalus maculipennis
To 17 in. (43 cm)

Winter plumage

Antarctic Tern
Sterna vittata
To 15 in. (38 cm)
Breeds in the Antarctic.

Arctic Tern
Sterna paradisaea
To 15 in. (38 cm)
Breeds in the Arctic and winters in the Antarctic. Migrates over 44,000 miles (70,000 km) each year, the longest migration route of any animal on Earth.

Rock Shag
Phalacrocorax magellanicus
To 3 ft. (90 cm)
Common in southern South America and the Falkland Islands, it is known locally as the black shag.

LAND & NEARSHORE BIRDS

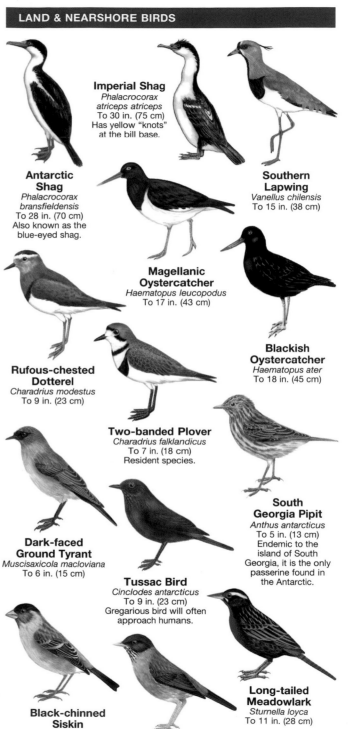

Imperial Shag
Phalacrocorax atriceps atriceps
To 30 in. (75 cm)
Has yellow "knots" at the bill base.

Antarctic Shag
Phalacrocorax bransfieldensis
To 28 in. (71 cm)
Also known as the blue-eyed shag.

Southern Lapwing
Vanellus chilensis
To 15 in. (38 cm)

Magellanic Oystercatcher
Haematopus leucopodus
To 17 in. (43 cm)

Rufous-chested Dotterel
Charadrius modestus
To 9 in. (23 cm)

Blackish Oystercatcher
Haematopus ater
To 18 in. (45 cm)

Two-banded Plover
Charadrius falklandicus
To 7 in. (18 cm)
Resident species.

South Georgia Pipit
Anthus antarcticus
To 5 in. (13 cm)
Endemic to the island of South Georgia, it is the only passerine found in the Antarctic.

Dark-faced Ground Tyrant
Muscisaxicola macloviana
To 6 in. (15 cm)

Tussac Bird
Cinclodes antarcticus
To 9 in. (23 cm)
Gregarious bird will often approach humans.

Black-chinned Siskin
Spinus barbatus
To 6 in. (15 cm)

Long-tailed Meadowlark
Sturnella loyca
To 11 in. (28 cm)

Falkland Thrush
Turdus falcklandii
To 10 in. (25 cm)

LAND & NEARSHORE BIRDS

Black-throated Finch
Melanodera melanodera
To 6 in. (15 cm)

Striated Caracara
Phalcoboenus australis
To 26 in. (65 cm)
Most numerous in the Falkland Islands.

Red-backed Hawk
Buteo polyosoma
To 25 in. (63 cm)
Also called buzzard.

SEABIRDS

Tubenoses – Order Procellariiformes
This order of seabirds includes four families: albatrosses, shearwaters and petrels, storm-petrels and diving-petrels. All species have nasal tubes on the upper bill and hooked beaks. The external nasal tubes enhance their sense of smell, allowing them to locate both prey in the water and their distant breeding colonies. They live at sea and only come on land to breed.

On albatrosses, the nostril tubes lie on either side of the bill.

On petrels, the tubes are fused at the bill base.

Albatrosses – Family Diomedeidae
Noted for their enormous wingspans, they glide low over waves with wings held stiffly.

Black-browed Albatross
Thalassarche melanophris
To 3 ft. (90 cm)
Has a blackish eyebrow and tail. Yellow bill has a pinkish tip. The most common and widespread albatross.

Gray-headed Albatross
Thalassarche chrysostoma
To 32 in. (80 cm)
Has gray head and blackish upper wings and tail. Black bill has a yellow line on the top.

Wandering Albatross
Diomedea exulans
To 53 in. (1.35 m)
Huge seabird has a large pink bill, pink feet and a wingspan of up to 11 ft. (3.3 m).

Light-mantled Albatross
Phoebetria palpebrata
To 3 ft. (90 cm)
Sooty brown to black bird has a dark head and a lighter back.

Southern Royal Albatross
Diomedea epomophora
To 4 ft. (1.2 m)
Has pale pink bill and feet and a clean, black and white appearance.

SEABIRDS

Fulmars, Shearwaters, Petrels & Prions – Family Procellariidae
These birds are distinguished by their flight pattern, several deep wingbeats followed by a long, low glide over waves. Shearwaters are distinguished from fulmars by their narrower wings and tail and longer, thinner bills. They feed on fish, squid and crustaceans in addition to carrion from fishing vessels.

Southern Fulmar
Fulmarus glacialoides
To 20 in. (50 cm)
Stocky gull-like bird is distinguished from gulls by its flight pattern.

Sooty Shearwater
Puffinus griseus To 18 in. (45 cm)
Has dark plumage, bill and feet. Has a shearing flight pattern, dipping from side to side as it glides – stiff-winged – like a black albatross.

Flesh-footed Shearwater
Puffinus carneipes
To 18 in. (45 cm)
All-dark bird has a black-tipped pinkish bill and pink legs and feet.

Southern Giant Petrel
Macronectes giganteus
To 3 ft. (90 cm)
Albatross-like bird has a pale band along leading edge of its wings. Also occurs in an all-white morph.

Northern Giant Petrel
Macronectes halli To 3 ft. (90 cm)
Underparts are darker than the southern giant petrel. Bill tip is pinkish.

Cape Petrel
Daption capense To 16 in. (40 cm)
White band on trailing edges of wings is less defined and has a "spattered paint" effect.

Antarctic Petrel
Thalassoica antarctica To 40 in. (1 m)
Distinguished by brown upperwings contrasting sharply with a broad white band on the trailing edge.

White-headed Petrel
Pterodroma lessonii
To 18 in. (45 cm)
Note white head and tail and dark eye patch.

Snow Petrel
Pagodroma nivea To 14 in. (35 cm)
All-white plumage is distinctive. One of only three birds (including the emperor and adelie penguins) to breed exclusively in Antarctica.

SEABIRDS

Mottled Petrel
Pterodroma inexpectata
To 14 in. (35 cm)
Distinguished by gray belly and large diagonal black stripe on underside of wings.

Soft-plumaged Petrel
Pterodroma mollis To 14 in. (35 cm)
Has a dark face mask and a dark breast band.

White-chinned Petrel
Procellaria aequinoctialis To 23 in. (58 cm)
Distinguished by dark plumage, ivory-colored bill and white chin. Larger than similar shearwaters.

Prions & Blue Petrel
Group of small petrels are blue-gray above and white below. All feed on small crustaceans and fish. Three species have flattened bills with specialized ridges that allow them to strain plankton from the water.

Broad-billed Prion
Pachyptila vittata
To 12 in. (30 cm)
Note stout bill and strong facial markings.

Fairy Prion
Pachyptila turtur
To 11 in. (28 cm)
Has less defined facial markings than the broad-billed prion.

Blue Petrel
Halobaena caerulea
To 12 in. (30 cm)
Note white forehead and blackish crown.

Slender-billed Prion
Pachyptila belcheri
To 11 in. (28 cm)
Key field mark is gray eye stripe.

Diving-Petrels – Family Pelecanoididae
Short-necked, short-winged, stocky birds are black above and white below. They have a characteristic whirring flight and fly through the water and air with equal ease. They dive as deep as 200 ft. (60 m) in search of crustaceans and plankton.

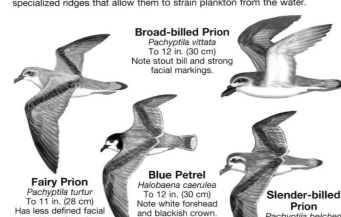

South Georgian Diving-petrel
Pelecanoides georgicus
To 8 in. (20 cm)

Common Diving-petrel
Pelecanoides urinatrix
To 10 in. (25 cm)
Has a narrower bill than the South Georgian species.

SEABIRDS

Storm-Petrels – Family Hydrobatidae
These small birds flutter and hop over waves with their legs dangling, often pattering the water's surface with their webbed feet as they pluck out small fish and plankton.

Wilson's Storm-Petrel
Oceanites oceanicus
To 7 in. (18 cm)
Sooty brown bird has a prominent white rump.

Black-bellied Storm-petrel
Fregetta tropica
To 11 in. (28 cm)

White-faced Storm-Petrel
Pelagodroma marina
To 8 in. (20 cm)

Gray-backed Storm-petrel
Garrodia nereis
To 11 in. (28 cm)
Back and upper tail are grayish.

Skuas & Jaegers – Order Charadriiformes Family Stercorariidae
Large, heavily-built dark birds are gull-like in appearance but have hooked bills and the predatory nature of a hawk. They feed on carrion, fish, birds, offal and often steal prey from other species. Most have light underwing patches at the base of the primaries.

South Polar Skua
Stercorarius maccormicki
To 21 in. (53 cm)
Has a pale nape and underparts.

Brown Skua
Stercorarius antarctica
To 26 in. (65 cm)
Upperwings are darker with a white patch at the base of the primaries.

Long-tailed Jaeger
Stercorarius longicaudus
To 2 ft. (60 cm)
Arctic breeder regularly winters in the Antarctic.

ANTARCTIC CODE OF CONDUCT
- Keep a safe distance from wildlife at land and at sea.
- When photographing animals, do not crowd them or cause them to alter their natural behavior.
- Do not disturb, feed or touch wildlife.
- Do not damage plants by walking on moss beds or stepping on lichens.
- Do not remove any items from historic sites or monuments including man-made items, rocks, bones, eggs or fossils.
- Be aware of restricted areas that have been afforded special protection.
- Do not disturb or remove scientific equipment.

SEASHORE LIFE

Red Crowberry
Empetrum rubrum
To 13 in. (33 cm)
Often the dominant plant in lowland shrub-heath areas.

Antarctic Pearlwort
Colobanthus quitensis
To 2 in. (5 cm)
Native plant has yellow flowers that bloom around Christmas.

Antarctic Hair Grass
Deschampsia antarctica
To 1 in. (3 cm)
One of two flowering plants native to Antarctica (south of 56° latitude).

Tussock Grass
Poa flabellata
To 6.5 ft. (2 m)
Long-lived grass grows in dense clumps in wet coastal areas and is a valuable source of shelter for a variety of animals.

Sea Cabbage
Senecio candicans
To 40 in. (1 m)
Common plant found above the tideline.

FISHES, ETC.
Over 200 species of fish inhabit Antarctic waters. Many species have antifreeze proteins in their blood to prevent them from freezing in subzero waters.

Pike Icefish
Champsocephalus esox
To 14 in. (33 cm)

Antarctic Toothfish
Dissostichus mawsoni
To 6.5 ft. (2 m)
One of the largest Antarctic fishes.

Bald Notothen
Pagothenia borchgrevinki
To 11 in. (28 cm)

Antarctic Cod
Notothenia coriiceps
To 5 ft. (1.5 m)

Crocodile Dragon Fish
Pseudochaenichthys georgianus
To 20 in. (50 cm)

Antarctic Spiny Plunderfish
Harpagifer antarcticus
To 4 in. (10 cm)
Often found in tide pools.

Colossal Squid
Mesonychoteuthis hamiltoni
To 45 ft. (13.5 m)
A major prey item for sperm whales, this deep-water species is rarely seen. The huge beaks of mature adults are often found in the stomachs of harvested whales.

Antarctic Krill
Euphausia superba
To 2.5 in. (6 cm)
The keystone species of the Antarctic food chain.

MARINE MAMMALS

Crabeater Seal
Lobodon carcinophagus To 7.5 ft. (2.3 m)
The most common Antarctic seal does not eat crabs; it has interlocking teeth which it uses to strain krill from the water.

Antarctic Fur Seal
Arctocephalus gazella
To 6.5 ft. (2 m)
Males are dark brown; females and juveniles are grayish.

Weddell Seal
Leptonychotes weddellii
To 12 ft. (3.6 m)
Note mottled coat.

Ross Seal
Ommatophoca rossii To 6.5 ft. (2 m)
Note large eyes.

Southern Elephant Seal
Mirounga leonina To 20 ft. (6 m)
Has a huge over-hanging snout.

Leopard Seal
Hydrurga leptonyx To 12 ft. (3.6 m)
Top predator feeds on fish, penguins and other seals.

Common Dolphin
Delphinus delphis
To 9 ft. (2.7 m)

Hourglass Dolphin
Lagenorhynchus cruciger
To 6 ft. (1.8 m)

Long-finned Pilot Whale
Globicephala melas
To 20 ft. (6 m)

Arnoux's Beaked Whale
Berardius arnuxii
To 40 ft. (12 m)

Southern Bottlenose Whale
Hyperoodon planifrons
To 25 ft. (7.6 m)

Antarctic Minke Whale
Balaenoptera bonaerensis
To 40 ft. (12 m)

MARINE MAMMALS

Humpback Whale
Megaptera novaeangliae
To 50 ft. (15 m)
Long flippers have "scalloped" edges.

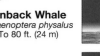

Sperm Whale
Physeter macrocephalus
To 70 ft. (21 m)

Sei Whale
Balaenoptera borealis
To 65 ft. (20 m)

Southern Right Whale
Eubalaena australis
To 50 ft. (15 m)

Blue Whale
Balaenoptera musculus
To 100 ft. (30 m)

Finback Whale
Balaenoptera physalus
To 80 ft. (24 m)

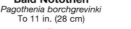

Killer Whale
Orcinus orca
To 30 ft. (9 m)
Not a true whale, it is related to dolphins.